QUINTESSENTIAL
PLEASURES

REFLECTIONS ON THE SIMPLE JOYS OF LIFE

THE METROPOLITAN MUSEUM OF ART
NEW YORK

CROWN PUBLISHERS, INC.
NEW YORK

Jacket: *The Monet Family in Their Garden*
Édouard Manet, French, 1832–1883
Oil on canvas
Bequest of Joan Whitney Payson, 1975   1976.201.14

Cover: Adapted from a Japanese stencil
Mulberry bark paper (*shibugami*) and thread,
late 19th–early 20th century
Gift of Miss D. Lorraine Yerkes, 1959   1975.90.6

Title page: *Willow Pond*
Catherine Wiley, American, 1879–1958
Oil on canvas, 1914
Gift of Mr. and Mrs. John Ernest Wiley, 1972   1972.114

Page 5: *A Cosey Corner*
Frank Millet, American, 1846–1912
Oil on canvas, 1884
Gift of George I. Seney, 1887   87.83

Produced by the Department of Special Publications,
The Metropolitan Museum of Art
Designed by Miriam Berman
Printed and bound in Singapore

Library of Congress Catalog Card Number: 92-083846
ISBN 0-87099-658-4 (MMA)
ISBN 0-517-59428-5 (Crown)
10 9 8 7 6 5 4 3 2
First Edition

INTRODUCTION

"Do any human beings ever realize life while they live it?—every, every minute?" asks Emily in Thornton Wilder's *Our Town*. Now a ghost, she laments the joys of a daily life that once seemed humdrum. And in fact, our lives are filled with agreeable activities that we seldom stop to contemplate. Great events and serious achievements are certainly important, but quiet moments of contentment or small unexpected delights also bring pleasure to our lives: receiving a letter in the mail, picking a bunch of wildflowers, making music with a friend, taking a midday nap, or simply doing nothing at all.

Thinkers, wits, and wags through the ages have recognized the importance of such pleasures. Sir John Lubbock, Lord Avebury, who wrote an entire book called *Peace and Happiness*, said, "The true pleasures are almost innumerable. Relations and friends, conversation, music, poetry, art, exercise and rest, the beauty and variety of nature, summer and winter, morning and evening, day and night, sunshine and storm, woods and fields, rivers and lakes and seas, animals and plants, trees and flowers, leaves and fruit, are but a few of them." Other writers focus on specific diversions, and some of their words are found in the pages that follow. The great statesmen Thomas Jefferson and Winston Churchill note that quiet pastimes balance their eventful lives. Emerson and Thoreau, as we might expect, extol the joys of solitude and of nature. And the eminent clergymen-poets John Donne and George Herbert find themselves restored by a letter or a shady tree. Such keen observers of human nature as Jane Austen, George Eliot, and Henry James pinpoint precise moments of enjoyment.

Fine artists, too, have been inspired to record life's simple pleasures. Rococo painters of hedonistic eighteenth-century France—Boucher, Fragonard, and Robert—created lighthearted pictures of courtiers at play. American artists of the nineteenth century revered nature and the common man, and the works here by Homer, Chase, and Sargent, among others, depict ordinary people and pleasant surroundings. The Impressionists, active in a time when leisure was no longer the privilege of the upper classes and when modern life was considered a fitting subject for artists, truly capture the spirit of these pleasant pursuits: Just looking at one of Monet's sun-filled scenes makes us feel relaxed and contented.

Sometimes it seems as if the tiresome thing about life is its "dailiness," the problems, chores, and anxieties that we face every day. Yet, as the pictures and quotations assembled in this book remind us, each day presents opportunities for countless pleasures, as well. And as the writer Kathleen Norris suggests: "Just the knowledge that a good book is awaiting one at the end of a long day makes that day happier."

CAROLYN VAUGHAN

G od Almighty
first planted a
garden. And,
indeed, it is the
purest of human
pleasures.

FRANCIS BACON
(1561–1626)

The Monet Family
in Their Garden
Édouard Manet
French, 1832–1883
Oil on canvas
Bequest of
Joan Whitney
Payson, 1975
1976.201.14

There are few hours in life more agreeable than the hour dedicated to the ceremony known as afternoon tea.

HENRY JAMES
(1843–1916)

Tea Leaves
William McGregor Paxton
American, 1869–1941
Oil on canvas, 1909
Gift of George A. Hearn, 1910
10.64.8

The sky is the daily bread of the eyes.

RALPH WALDO EMERSON
(1803–1882)

Twilight on the Sound,
Darien, Connecticut
John Frederick Kensett
American, 1816–1872
Oil on canvas, 1872
Gift of Thomas
Kensett, 1874
74.24

Teach us delight in simple things.

RUDYARD KIPLING
(1865–1936)

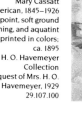

Feeding the Ducks
Mary Cassatt
American, 1845–1926
Drypoint, soft ground
etching, and aquatint
printed in colors;
ca. 1895
H. O. Havemeyer
Collection
Bequest of Mrs. H. O.
Havemeyer, 1929
29.107.100

Music washes away from the soul the dust of everyday life.

BERTHOLD AUERBACH
(1812–1882)

Two Young Girls at the Piano
Pierre-Auguste Renoir
French, 1841–1919
Oil on canvas
Robert Lehman
Collection, 1975
1975.1.201

No occupation is so delightful to me as the culture of the earth, and no culture comparable to that of the garden.... But though an old man, I am but a young gardener.

THOMAS JEFFERSON
(1743–1826)

The Gardener
Georges Seurat
French, 1859–1891
Oil on wood, 1882–83
Bequest of
Miss Adelaide
Milton de Groot
(1876–1967), 1967
67.187.102

Just to paint is great fun. The colours are lovely to look at and delicious to squeeze out. Matching them, however crudely, with what you see is fascinating and absolutely absorbing. Try it if you have not done so—before you die.

SIR WINSTON CHURCHILL
(1874–1965)

Great trees are good for nothing but shade.

GEORGE HERBERT
(1593–1633)

The Bodmer Oak,
Fontainebleau Forest
Claude Monet
French, 1840–1926
Oil on canvas
Gift of Sam Salz and
Bequest of
Julia W. Emmons,
by exchange, 1964
64.210

I frequently tramped eight or ten miles through the deepest snow to keep an appointment with a beech tree, or a yellow birch, or an old acquaintance among the pines.

HENRY DAVID THOREAU
(1817–1862)

The sunshine seemed to bless,
The air was a caress.

JOHN GREENLEAF WHITTIER (1807–1892)

At the Seaside
William Merritt Chase, American, 1849–1916
Oil on canvas, ca. 1892
Bequest of Miss Adelaide Milton de Groot (1876–1967), 1967
67.187.123

I loafe and invite my soul . . .

WALT WHITMAN
(1819–1892)

Figure in Hammock, Florida
John Singer Sargent
American, 1856–1925
Watercolor on paper,
1895
Gift of Mrs. Francis
Ormond, 1950
50.130.57

The habit of reading is the only enjoyment in which there is no alloy; it lasts when all other pleasures fade.

ANTHONY TROLLOPE
(1815–1882)

A quiet heart is a continual feast.

PROVERBS 15:15

Madame Arthur Fontaine
Odilon Redon
French, 1840–1916
Pastel on paper, 1901
The Mr. and Mrs.
Henry Ittleson, Jr.
Purchase Fund, 1960
60.54

I have laid aside business, and gone a-fishing.

IZAAK WALTON
(1593–1683)

Early June Landscape
Paul-Désiré Trouillebert
French, 1829–1900
Oil on canvas
Robert Lehman
Collection, 1975
1975.1.212

I always felt that the great
high privilege, relief and
comfort of friendship was that
one had to explain nothing.

KATHERINE MANSFIELD
(1888–1923)

Two Girls on a Lawn
John Singer Sargent
American, 1856–1925
Oil on canvas, ca. 1889
Gift of Mrs. Francis
Ormond, 1950
50.130.20

35

The great pleasure of a dog is that you may make a fool of yourself with him and not only will he not scold you, but he will make a fool of himself too.

SAMUEL BUTLER
(1835–1902)

When from our better
  selves we have too long
Been parted by the
  hurrying world, and droop,
Sick of its business,
  of its pleasures tired,
How gracious, how benign,
  is Solitude.

WILLIAM WORDSWORTH
(1770–1850)

The Coming Storm
Martin Johnson Heade
American, 1819–1904
Oil on canvas, 1859
Gift of Erving Wolf
Foundation and Mr.
and Mrs. Erving Wolf,
1975
1975.160

I expand and live in the warm day like corn and melons.

RALPH WALDO EMERSON
(1803–1882)

Indian Summer
William Trost Richards
American, 1833–1905
Oil on canvas, 1875
Bequest of Collis P.
Huntington, 1900
25.110.6

In saffron-colored mantle
   from the tides
Of Ocean rose the Morning
   to bring light
To gods and men.

HOMER
(9th–8th century B.C.)

September Morn
Paul Chabas
French, 1869–1937
Oil on canvas, ca. 1912
Purchase, Mr. and
Mrs. William Coxe
Wright Gift, 1957
57.89

Where's the man could ease a heart
Like a satin gown?

DOROTHY PARKER
(1893–1967)

Before the Mirror
Pierre-Paul-Léon Glaize
French, 1842–1932
Oil on canvas, 1873
Catharine Lorillard
Wolfe Collection,
Bequest of Catharine
Lorillard Wolfe, 1887
87.15.74

Before green
    apples blush,
Before green
    nuts embrown,
Why, one day
    in the country
Is worth a month
    in town.

CHRISTINA ROSSETTI
(1830–1894)

Jallais Hill, Pontoise
Camille Pissarro
French, 1830–1903
Oil on canvas, 1867
Bequest of William
Church Osborn, 1951
51.30.2

A lunch of bread
and cheese after a
good walk is more
enjoyable than a
Lord Mayor's feast.

SIR JOHN LUBBOCK
(1834–1913)

Banks of the River Marne
Henri Cartier-Bresson
French, b. 1908
Gelatin silver print,
1938
Warner Communications, Inc.
Purchase Fund and Gift of
Creilly Pollack
in memory of
Peter Pollack, 1981
1981.1152.1

Midday slumbers are golden: they make the body fat, the skin fair, the flesh plump, delicate, and tender; they set a rusty color on the cheeks of young women, and make lusty courage to rise up in men.

THOMAS DEKKER
(1572?–1632)

The Interrupted Sleep
François Boucher
French, 1703–1770
Oil on canvas, 1750
The Jules Bache
Collection, 1949
49.7.46

It is perhaps a more fortunate destiny to have a taste for collecting shells than to be born a millionaire.

ROBERT LOUIS STEVENSON
(1850–1894)

Eagle Head,
Manchester,
Massachusetts
(*High Tide*)
Winslow Homer
American, 1836–1910
Oil on canvas, 1870
Gift of Mrs. William F.
Milton, 1923
23.77.2

M ore than kisses, letters mingle souls.

JOHN DONNE
(1572–1631)

When the spirits sink too low, the best cordial is to read over all the letters of one's friends.

WILLIAM SHENSTONE
(1714–1763)

Letters
Priscilla Roberts
American, b. 1916
Oil on canvas, 1956–57
Purchase, Elihu Root, Jr.
Gift, 1957
57.87

It is a great delight
to dwell in a picture.

D. H. LAWRENCE
(1885–1930)

*Study for "A Sunday on
La Grande Jatte"*
Georges Seurat
French, 1859–1891
Oil on canvas, 1884
Bequest of Sam A.
Lewisohn, 1951
51.112.6

Animals are such agreeable friends—
they ask no questions, they pass no
criticisms.

GEORGE ELIOT
(1819–1880)

Martha Bartlett
with Her Kitten
American, 1875–1900
Oil on canvas
Bequest of
Edgar William and
Bernice Chrysler
Garbisch, 1979
1980.341.11

A little Madness in the Spring
Is wholesome even for the King.

EMILY DICKINSON
(1830–1866)

Spring in Central Park
Adolf Dehn
American, b. 1895
Watercolor on paper,
1941
Fletcher Fund, 1941
41.113

63

It is not necessary to understand music; it is only necessary that one enjoy it.

LEOPOLD STOKOWSKI
(1882–1977)

Charleston on the Bauhaus Roof
Lux Feininger
American,
b. (Germany) 1910
Gelatin silver print,
1927
Ford Motor Company
Collection, Gift of
Ford Motor Company
and John C. Waddell,
1987
1987.1100.107

To sit in the shade on a fine day and look upon verdure is the most perfect refreshment.

JANE AUSTEN
(1775–1817)

The Parc Monceau
Claude Monet
French, 1840–1926
Oil on canvas, 1878
The Mr. and Mrs.
Henry Ittleson, Jr.
Purchase Fund, 1959
59.142

Animals are such agreeable friends—
they ask no questions, they pass no
criticisms.

GEORGE ELIOT
(1819–1880)

Martha Bartlett
with Her Kitten
American, 1875–1900
Oil on canvas
Bequest of
Edgar William and
Bernice Chrysler
Garbisch, 1979
1980.341.11

It is a great delight
to dwell in a picture.

D. H. LAWRENCE
(1885–1930)

*Study for "A Sunday on
La Grande Jatte"*
Georges Seurat
French, 1859–1891
Oil on canvas, 1884
Bequest of Sam A.
Lewisohn, 1951
51.112.6

When the spirits sink too low, the best cordial is to read over all the letters of one's friends.

WILLIAM SHENSTONE
(1714–1763)

Letters
Priscilla Roberts
American, b. 1916
Oil on canvas, 1956–57
Purchase, Elihu Root, Jr.
Gift, 1957
57.87

More than kisses, letters mingle souls.

JOHN DONNE
(1572–1631)

It is perhaps a more fortunate destiny to have a taste for collecting shells than to be born a millionaire.

ROBERT LOUIS STEVENSON
(1850–1894)

Eagle Head,
Manchester,
Massachusetts
(*High Tide*)
Winslow Homer
American, 1836–1910
Oil on canvas, 1870
Gift of Mrs. William F.
Milton, 1923
23.77.2

Midday slumbers are golden: they make the body fat, the skin fair, the flesh plump, delicate, and tender; they set a rusty color on the cheeks of young women, and make lusty courage to rise up in men.

THOMAS DEKKER
(1572?–1632)

The Interrupted Sleep
François Boucher
French, 1703–1770
Oil on canvas, 1750
The Jules Bache
Collection, 1949
49.7.46

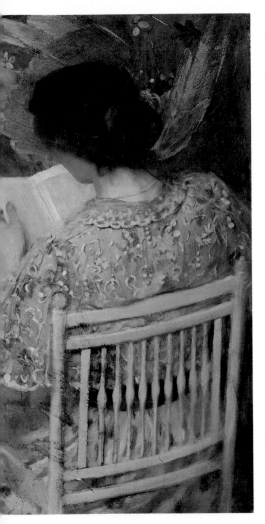

You may have tangible
    wealth untold;
Caskets of jewels
    and coffers of gold.
Richer than I
    you can never be—
I had a mother
    who read to me.

STRICKLAND GILLILAN
(1869–1954)

Jungle Tales
(*Contes de la Jungle*)
James J. Shannon
American, 1862–1923
Oil on canvas, 1895
Arthur Hoppock
Hearn Fund, 1913
13.143.1

69

Arranging a bowl of flowers in the morning can give a sense of quiet in a crowded day—like writing a poem, or saying a prayer.

ANNE MORROW LINDBERGH
(b. 1906)

Suzanne Valadon
1908

Noble deeds and hot baths are the best cures for depression.

DODIE SMITH
(b. 1896)

Blessings on him that first invented
sleep! It covers a man, thoughts and all,
like a cloak; it is meat for the hungry,
drink for the thirsty, heat for the cold, and
cold for the hot. It is the current coin that
purchases cheaply all the pleasures of
the world, and the balance that sets even
king and shepherd, fool and sage.

MIGUEL DE CERVANTES
(1547–1616)

The Harvesters (detail)
Pieter Bruegel the Elder
Flemish,
active by 1551, d. 1569
Oil on wood, 1565
Rogers Fund, 1919
19.164

He is happiest, be he king
or peasant, who finds peace
in his home.

JOHANN WOLFGANG VON GOETHE
(1749–1832)

Victorian Parlor II
Horace Pippin
American, 1888–1946
Oil on canvas, 1945
Arthur Hoppock
Hearn Fund, 1958
58.26

This is the best day the world has ever seen. Tomorrow will be better.

R. A. CAMPBELL

The Swing
Hubert Robert
French, 1733–1808
Oil on canvas
Gift of J. Pierpont
Morgan, 1917
17.190.27